# Ding Dong

by Frances Greter
illustrated by Meryl Henderson

Practice Decodable 44

I0805975

McGraw Hill Education

Bothell, WA • Chicago, IL • Columbus, OH • New York, NY

**MHEonline.com**



Send all inquiries to:
McGraw-Hill Education
8787 Orion Place
Columbus, OH 43240

ISBN: 978-0-02-133267-0
MHID: 0-02-133267-3

Printed in China.

8 9 10 11 12 DSS 27 26 25 24 23

Ding dong! Ding dong!
"Is that the bell?" asked Nick.

"Let's swing on the swing set," said Amber.

"Can I bring King?" asked Nick.
"But what can he do?" asked Amber.

"King can fetch long sticks," said Nick.

"Fling that thing!" said Amber.
"Fetch the stick, King!" said Nick.

"Mom is ringing the dinner bell.
I better get back," said Nick.